Pocket Poems

SELECTED BY *Bobbi Katz* ✻ ILLUSTRATED BY *Marylin Hafner*

PUFFIN BOOKS
An Imprint of Penguin Group (USA) Inc.

PUFFIN BOOKS
Published by the Penguin Group
Penguin Young Readers Group, 345 Hudson Street, New York, New York 10014, U.S.A.
Penguin Group (Canada), 90 Eglinton Avenue East, Suite 700, Toronto, Ontario M4P 2Y3, Canada
(a division of Pearson Penguin Canada Inc.)
Penguin Books Ltd, 80 Strand, London WC2R 0RL, England
Penguin Ireland, 25 St Stephen's Green, Dublin 2, Ireland (a division of Penguin Books Ltd)
Penguin Group (Australia), 707 Collins St., Melbourne, Victoria 3008, Australia
(a division of Pearson Australia Group Pty Ltd)
Penguin Books India Pvt Ltd, 11 Community Centre, Panchsheel Park, New Delhi–110 017, India
Penguin Group (NZ), 67 Apollo Drive, Rosedale, Auckland 0632, New Zealand
(a division of Pearson New Zealand Ltd)
Penguin Books, Rosebank Office Park, 181 Jan Smuts Avenue, Parktown North 2193, South Africa
Penguin China, B7 Jiaming Center, 27 East Third Ring Road North, Chaoyang District, Beijing 100020, China

Penguin Books Ltd, Registered Offices: 80 Strand, London WC2R 0RL, England

First published in the United States of America by Dutton Children's Books,
a division of Penguin Young Readers Group, 2004
Published by Puffin Books, a member of Penguin Young Readers Group, 2013

5 7 9 10 8 6 4

THE LIBRARY OF CONGRESS HAS CATALOGED THE DUTTON CHILDREN'S BOOKS EDITION AS FOLLOWS:
Katz, Bobbi.
Pocket poems / selected by Bobbi Katz ; illustrated by Marylin Hafner.
p. cm.
Summary: A collection of short poems by such authors as: Gwendolyn Brooks, Emily Dickinson, Emily George,
Nikki Giovanni, Eve Merriam, and Charlotte Pomerantz.
ISBN 978-0-525-47172-1 (hc)
[1. Children's poetry—American. 2. American poetry—Collections.] I. Title.
PS586.3.P6342004 [811.008/09282]—dc28 2003060667

Puffin Books ISBN 978-0-14-750859-1

Manufactured in China

ALWAYS LEARNING   PEARSON

For Lucia and Jennifer

—B.K.

For Abby, Doug, Jennifer, Linda,
Herman, and Amanda, with love

—M.H.

ACKNOWLEDGMENTS

Every attempt has been made to trace the ownership of all copyrighted material and to secure the necessary permissions
to reprint these selections. In the event of any question arising as to the use of any material, the editor and the publisher,
while expressing regret for any inadvertent error, will be happy to make the necessary correction in future printings.

THE PUBLISHER GRATEFULLY ACKNOWLEDGES:

Robin Bernard for "Brush Dance." Copyright © 2004 by Robin Bernard. ✶ Shirlee Curlee Bingham for excerpt from
"English Is a Pain! (Pane?)." Copyright © 1994 by Shirlee Curlee Bingham. ✶ Candlewick Press, Inc., Cambridge, Mass.,
on behalf of Walker Books Ltd., London, for "That's the Way To Do It!" from *Who's Been Sleeping in My Porridge? A
Book of Wacky Poems and Pictures.* Copyright © 1990 by Colin McNaughton. Reprinted with permission. ✶ William
Cole for "Banananananananana." Copyright © 1977 by William Cole. ✶ Mittie Cuetara for "The Dog Show." Copyright
© 1997 by Mittie Cuetara and reprinted with her permission. ✶ Curtis Brown Ltd. for "Sea Horse and Sawhorse," from
One Winter Night in August and Other Nonsense Jingles. Copyright © 1975 by X. J. Kennedy. "January" by Lucille
Clifton. Copyright © 1971 by Lucille Clifton. Reprinted by permission of Curtis Brown Ltd. ✶ Dutton Children's Books
for excerpt from "Moonwalker," from *Lunch Money* by Carol Diggory Shields. Text copyright © 1995 by Carol Diggory
Shields. Reprinted by permission of Dutton Children's Books, a member of Penguin Putnam Inc. ✶ Farrar, Straus and
Giroux for "the drum," from *Spin a Soft Black Song* by Nikki Giovanni. Copyright © 1971, 1985 by Nikki Giovanni.
Reprinted by Hill and Wang, a division of Farrar, Straus and Giroux, LLC. "Lunchbox" by Valerie Worth. Copyright ©
1987, 1994 by Valerie Worth. Reprinted by permission of Farrar, Straus and Giroux, LLC. ✶ Betsy Franco for "At the Bike
Rack." Copyright © 2004 by Betsy Franco. ✶ Emily George for "To Start a Day Aliona's Way," "Aliona Says," "Aliona's
Street," "Aliona Sees," and "Silly Aliona." Copyright © 2004. ✶ Isabel Joshlin Glaser for "Writing on the Chalkboard."
Copyright © 1987. Used by permission of the author, who controls all rights. ✶ Sandra Guy for "Evening." Copyright ©
2004 by Sandra Guy. ✶ Harcourt, Inc. for excerpt from "Arithmetic" in *The People, Yes* by Carl Sandburg. Copyright ©
1936 by Harcourt, Inc. and renewed 1964 by Carl Sandburg. Reprinted by permission of the publisher. ✶ HarperCollins
Publishers for "Robert, Who Is Often a Stranger to Himself," from *Bronzeville Boys and Girls.* Text copyright © 1956 by
Gwendolyn Brooks Blakely. "You—Tú," from *The Tamarindo Puppy.* Text copyright © 1960 by Charlotte Pomerantz.
"The World's Fastest Turtle," from *It's Raining Pigs and Noodles.* Text copyright © 2000 by Jack Prelutsky. Used by per-
mission of HarperCollins Publishers. ✶ Highlights for Children for excerpt from "Toothpaste" by Stan Lee Werlin, from
the October 1995 issue of *Highlights for Children* magazine. Copyright © 1995 by Highlights for Children, Inc.,
Columbus, Ohio. ✶ Bobbi Katz for "A Pocket Poem" and "Cat Profile," copyright © 2004 by Bobbi Katz; excerpts from
"Did You Ever Think?," copyright © 1981 and "Spring Conversations," copyright © 2001 by Bobbi Katz; "The Period" and
"The Question Mark," copyright © 1999 by Bobbi Katz. Used by permission of bobbikatz@aol.com. ✶ Monica Kulling for
"Hop to It!" and "Call Me Polar Bear." Copyright © 2004 by Monica Kulling. Used by permission of the author. ✶
J. Patrick Lewis for "Home Poem (Or, The Sad Dog Song)," from *Ridicholas Nicholas: More Animal Poems.* Text copyright
© 1995 by J. Patrick Lewis and reprinted with his permission. ✶ Margaret K. McElderry Books for "Feet Talk," from *A
Crack in the Clouds* by Constance Levy. Copyright © 1998 by Constance Levy. Reprinted by permission of Margaret K.
McElderry Books, an imprint of Simon & Schuster Children's Publishing Division. ✶ Random House, Inc. for "Bedroom
Window," from *Wake Up, House! Rooms Full of Poems* by Dee Lillegard. Text copyright © 2000 by Dee Lillegard. Used
by permission of Alfred A. Knopf, an imprint of Random House Children's Books. ✶ Marian Reiner for "A Robin," from
Feathered Ones and Furry by Aileen Fisher. Text copyright © 1971, 1999 by Aileen Fisher. "Hurry" by Eve Merriam, from
The Singing Green by Eve Merriam. Text copyright © 1992. Estate of Eve Merriam; Marian Reiner, Literary Executor.
"Dragon Smoke," from *I Feel the Same Way* by Lilian Moore. Text copyright © 1967, 1995 by Lilian Moore. "Keep a Poem
in Your Pocket," from *Something Special* by Beatrice Schenk de Regniers. Text copyright © 1958, 1986. Used by permis-
sion of Marian Reiner. ✶ Jo Roberts for "My Snake." Copyright © 2004. ✶ Westwood Creative Artists for "Dickery
Dean," from *Jelly Belly* (Macmillan of Canada) by Dennis Lee. Text copyright © 1983 by Dennis Lee. Used by permission.

CONTENTS

A POCKET POEM

With a poem in your pocket
and
a pocket in your pants
you can rock with new rhythms.
You can skip.
You can dance.
And wherever you go,
and whatever you do,
that poem in your pocket is going there, too.
You could misplace your homework.
You could lose your left shoe.
But that poem in your pocket will be part of you.
And nothing can take it.
And nothing can break it.
That poem in your pocket
becomes
part of . . .
YOU!

Bobbi Katz

I'M GLAD

I'm glad the sky is painted blue,

And earth is painted green,
With such a lot of nice fresh air
All sandwiched in between.

Anonymous

BEDROOM WINDOW

Sun rises
lights the sky
shines through the window's
open eye.

Dee Lillegard

TO START A DAY ALIONA'S WAY

S
T
R
E
T
C
H
from
your head
to the tips
of your toes.
Check on the weather.
Slip
into your clothes.

Emily George

AUTUMN

The morns are meeker than they were,
The berry's cheek is plumper,
The nuts are getting brown;
The rose is out of town.

The maple wears a gayer scarf,
The field a scarlet gown.
Lest I should be old-fashioned
I'll put a trinket on.

Emily Dickinson

JACK FROST

Someone painted pictures on my
Window pane last night—
Willow trees with trailing boughs
And flowers—frosty white
And lovely crystal butterflies;
But when the morning sun
Touched them with its golden beams,
They vanished one by one!

Helen Bayley Davis

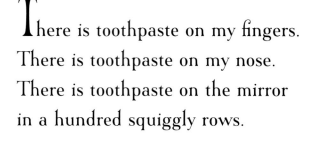

FROM
TOOTHPASTE

There is toothpaste on my fingers.
There is toothpaste on my nose.
There is toothpaste on the mirror
in a hundred squiggly rows.

Every time I squeeze the toothpaste,
it sprays north and west and south.
There is toothpaste almost everywhere,
except inside my mouth!

Stan Lee Werlin

ROBERT, WHO IS OFTEN
A STRANGER TO HIMSELF

Do you ever look in the looking-glass
And see a stranger there?
A child you know and do not know,
Wearing what you wear?

Gwendolyn Brooks

* 4 *

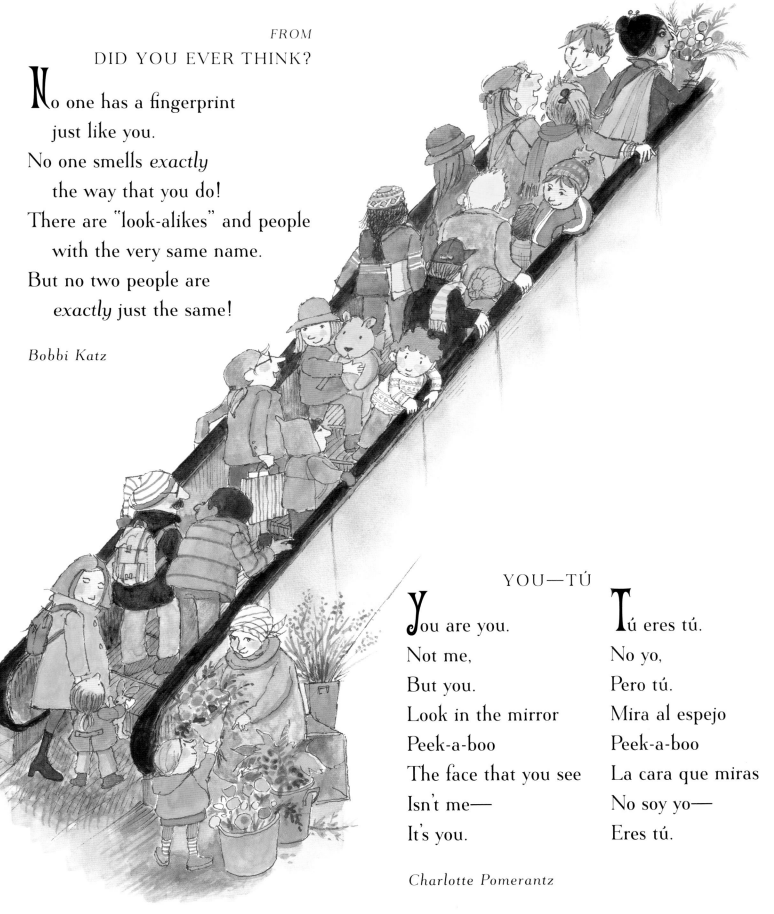

DID YOU EVER THINK?

No one has a fingerprint
    just like you.
No one smells *exactly*
    the way that you do!
There are "look-alikes" and people
    with the very same name.
But no two people are
    exactly just the same!

Bobbi Katz

YOU—TÚ

You are you.
Not me,
But you.
Look in the mirror
Peek-a-boo
The face that you see
Isn't me—
It's you.

Tú eres tú.
No yo,
Pero tú.
Mira al espejo
Peek-a-boo
La cara que miras
No soy yo—
Eres tú.

Charlotte Pomerantz

BREAKFAST

Humpty Dumpty sat on a wall.
Humpty Dumpty had a great fall.
Then all the King's horses
And all the King's men
Had scrambled eggs
For breakfast again.

Anonymous

"Walk tall in the world,"
says Mama
to Everett Anderson.
"The year is new and
so are the days,
walk tall in the world,"
she says.

Lucille Clifton

the drum

daddy says the world is
a drum tight and hard
and i told him
i'm gonna beat
out my own rhythm

Nikki Giovanni

ALIONA SAYS

An off-to-school hug
is quick but nice.
Mine always comes
with some words
of advice.

Emily George

* 7 *

FEET TALK

Listen as your feet
tell you where they walk:
    gravel crackles,
    grass squeaks,
    sneaker slaps
    on hard concrete.
Tune in to
    friendly chitchat
    of feet meeting feet:
        hurried shuffles, clacks, thumps
        crossing busy streets.
    Hear your feet talk
    street talk!

Constance Levy

DRAGON SMOKE

Breathe and blow
white clouds
    with every puff.
It's cold today,
    cold enough
to see your breath.
Huff!
    Breathe dragon smoke
    today!

Lilian Moore

CALL ME POLAR BEAR

I trudge to school
like a polar bear
breathing out clouds
of frosty air

Some people say
winter's a song
but bears don't sing
they just plod along

Monica Kulling

ALIONA'S STREET

My street has a garden
neat and small
that tells me,
"It's summer."
"It's spring."
"It's fall."
But all winter long
it does not make a peep.
Please pass it on tiptoes.
The plants are asleep.

Emily George

FROM ENGLISH IS A PAIN! (PANE?)

Rain, reign, rein,
English is a pain.
Although the words
sound just alike,
the spelling's not the same!

There, their, they're,
enough to make you swear.
Too many ways
to write one sound,
I just don't think it's fair!

To, two, too,
so what's a kid to do?
I think I'll go
to live on Mars,
and leave this mess with ewe!
(you?)

Shirlee Curlee Bingham

BANANANANANANANANA

I thought I'd win the spelling bee
And get right to the top,
But I started to spell "banana,"
And I didn't know when to stop.

William Cole

WRITING ON THE CHALKBOARD

Up and down, my chalk goes.
Squeak, squeak, squeak!
Hush, chalk.
Don't squawk.
Talk *softly* when you speak.

Isabel Joshlin Glaser

Arithmetic is where numbers fly like pigeons in and out of your head.

Arithmetic tells you how many you lose or win if you know how many you had before you lost or won.

Arithmetic is seven eleven all good children go to heaven—or five six bundle of sticks.

Arithmetic is numbers you squeeze from your head to your hand to your pencil to your paper till you get the answer.

Carl Sandburg

THE BURP

Pardon me for being rude.
It was not me, it was my food.
It got so lonely down below,
it just popped up to say hello.

Anonymous

LUNCHBOX

They always
End up
Fighting—

The soft
Square
Sandwich,

The round
Heavy
Apple.

Valerie Worth

FROM
SPRING CONVERSATIONS

"Whisk!"
whirls the jump rope,
        twirling
around.
        "Thud!"
say the sneakers,
        bouncing off the ground.

Bobbi Katz

HOP TO IT!

I draw a square
on top of a square
on top of a square
with chalk.

The stone has fling
my step has spring
I hop and I hop and
I hop.

Monica Kulling

AT THE BIKE RACK

When you leave your bike in the bike rack,
don't you wish you knew
if the bicycles talked to each other
and what your bike says about you?

Betsy Franco

THE PERIOD

The period is just a dot,
but it gets to do a lot.
A period goes at the end
each time you make a statement, friend.

Bobbi Katz

THE QUESTION MARK

When does a question mark appear?
When do you ask a question, dear?
What do question marks all show?
There's something someone wants to know.

Bobbi Katz

BRUSH DANCE

A dot,
a blot,
a smidge,
a smear,
and just a little squiggle here . . .

A dab,
a dash,
a splish,
a splat,
that's how Patrick paints a cat!

Robin Bernard

THE SQUIRREL

Whisky,
Frisky,
Hippity,
Hop,
Up he goes
To the treetop!
Whirly, twirly,
Round and round,
Down
He scampers
To the ground.
Where's his supper?
In the shell.
Snappity,
Crackity,
Out it fell!

Anonymous

A ROBIN

I wonder how
a robin hears?

I never yet
have seen his ears.

But I have seen him
cock his head,

And pull a worm
right out of bed.

Aileen Fisher

ALIONA SEES

If you walked home
From school with me,
You'd see the things
I get to see.

Emily George

FROM
MOONWALKER

I'm a moonwalker, walking on the moon.
I'm a jungle stalker, stalking wild baboons.
I'm a superhero, skimming through the blue.
Puddle jumping, leaf-pile leaping, I'm a kangaroo.

I'm a red-eyed robot, clanking up the road.
I'm an eighteen-wheeler with a heavy load.
I'm a famous rock star, moving very cool.
Actually,
     I'm just me,
          Walking home from school.

Carol Diggory Shields

SILLY ALIONA

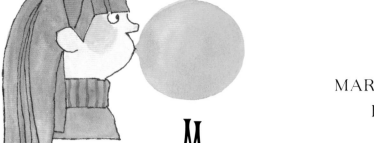

When silly rhymes
Go tick-tick-tickle,
Lickety-split
I'm in a pickle.
My funny bone
Starts wig-wig-wiggling.
Then quick-quick-quick
I'm gig-gig-giggling.

Emily George

MARY HAD SOME
BUBBLE GUM

Mary had some bubble gum,
She chewed it long and slow.
And everywhere that Mary went,
Her gum was sure to go.
She chewed the gum in school one day,
Which was against the rule.
The teacher took her pack away
And chewed it after school.

Anonymous

MARY HAD A
LITTLE LAMB

Mary had a little lamb,
You've heard this tale before;
But did you know
She passed her plate
And had a little more?

Anonymous

MORE,
PLEASE

THAT'S THE WAY
TO DO IT!

There was an old woman
  Who lived in a shoe;
She had so many children
  She didn't know what to do.
So she sought the advice
  Of her friend Mr. Punch,
Who said fry them with onions
  And eat them for lunch!

Colin McNaughton

Stay in Line, Children!

TWINKLE, TWINKLE

Twinkle, twinkle, little bat!
How I wonder what you're at!
Up above the world you fly,
Like a tea-tray in the sky.
     Twinkle, twinkle—

Lewis Carroll

DICKERY DEAN

"What's the matter
 With Dickery Dean?
He jumped right into
 The washing machine!"

"Nothing's the matter
 With Dickery Dean—
He dove in dirty,
 And he jumped out clean!"

Dennis Lee

RAISING FROGS
FOR PROFIT

Raising frogs for profit
Is a very sorry joke.
How can you make money
When so many of them croak?

Anonymous

HIGGLETY, PIGGLETY, POP

Higglety, pigglety, pop!
The dog has eaten the mop;
The pig's in a hurry,
The cat's in a flurry,
Higglety, pigglety, pop!

Samuel G. Goodrich

THE WORLD'S FASTEST TURTLE

The world's fastest turtle
and the world's slowest horse
raced one another
around a great course.

The horse won the race,
you'd expect that, of course…
a turtle's a turtle,
a horse is a horse.

Jack Prelutsky

SEA HORSE AND SAWHORSE

A sea horse saw a sawhorse
On a seesaw meant for two.
"See here, sawhorse," said sea horse,
"May I seesaw with you?"

"I'll see, sea horse," said sawhorse.
"Right now I'm having fun
Seeing if I'll be seasick
On a seesaw meant for one."

X. J. Kennedy

CAT PROFILE

Lucy's the name.
Hunting's my game.
I'm stalk,
pounce
and purr
packed in
whiskers
and fur.

Bobbi Katz

MY SNAKE

Let other kids have cats and dogs.
I love my pet snake Jake.
And Jake appreciates the frogs
That I catch in the lake.
It makes me sad each time I think
I'll have to let Jake go
Before the lake's a skating rink
And the fields are white with snow.

Jo Roberts

thanks!

THE DOG SHOW

Oscar's dog is very fat.
Lisa's dog looks like a rat.
Jane's is an aristocrat.
Leon's dog is…oops, a cat!

Mittie Cuetara

HOME POEM
(OR,
THE SAD DOG
SONG)

Home of the moth: cloth.
Home of the mole: hole.

Home of the bear: lair.
Home of the ants: pants.

Home of the gnu: zoo.
Home of the flea: me!

J. Patrick Lewis

MAGGY'S DOG

There was a young girl called Maggy,
Whose dog was enormous and shaggy.
    The front end of him
    Looked vicious and grim,
But the tail end was friendly and waggy.

Anonymous

EVENING

Evening listens to my music
Scraping her ear against the window
To catch every word of my song

Sandra Guy

HURRY

Hurry! says the morning,
don't be late for school!

Hurry! says the teacher,
hand in papers now!

Hurry! says the mother,
supper's getting cold!

Hurry! says the father,
time to go to bed!

Slowly, says the darkness,
you can talk to me . . .

Eve Merriam

FROM
NIGHT

The moon, like a flower
In heaven's high bower,
With silent delight
Sits and smiles on the night.

William Blake

HOME

All around me quiet.
All around me peaceful.
All around me lasting.
All around me home.

Ute Indian

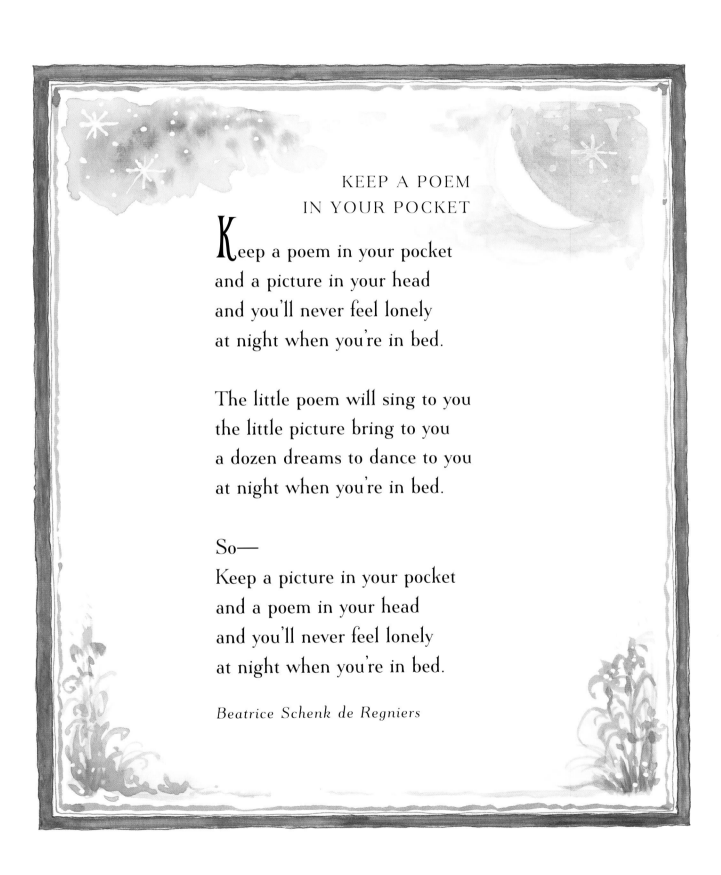

KEEP A POEM
IN YOUR POCKET

Keep a poem in your pocket
and a picture in your head
and you'll never feel lonely
at night when you're in bed.

The little poem will sing to you
the little picture bring to you
a dozen dreams to dance to you
at night when you're in bed.

So—
Keep a picture in your pocket
and a poem in your head
and you'll never feel lonely
at night when you're in bed.

Beatrice Schenk de Regniers

Thirty years ago, the very first collection of my own poems was titled
Upside Down and Inside Out: Poems for All Your Pockets. Now here
comes *Pocket Poems*, a brand-new anthology featuring the work of many
poets. In the years between these two books, I learned that teachers were
connecting poems and pockets in various ways. What makes two seemingly
different things such natural go-togethers? A pocket: A private place, a
personal place, a close-to-the-body place, a hiding place, a safe place to store
a small treasure or a key. A poem: A snapshot in words, a safe place to
express feelings, a close-to-the-heart place, a place where one might discover
a small treasure or . . . a key. A logic begins to emerge.

When we memorize poems, they become part of us. We own them forever.
Even on busy days, there's a moment to slip a poem out of a pocket. I've
selected short poems so that children can experience the sweet taste of
ownership easily. And most of the poems rhyme.

"Everyone likes rhyme," said Dr. Steven Pinker, the author of *The
Language Instinct*. Both gifted orators and rappers know that rhyme and
rhythm please. Dr. Pinker believes that rhyme resonates with the way the
human brain decodes the confusing avalanche of information the world
presents.

I'm sure that teachers, librarians, and parents don't need studies by
neurologists and psychologists to learn that the love of rhyme seems
instinctive. Nor do they need experts to prove that playing rhyming games
helps kids become better readers. Yet recent studies by the National Institute
for Child Health and Human Development and the Center for Cognitive
Studies at the Massachusetts Institute of Technology provide scientific data to
assure us that as we welcome poetry into our homes, our classrooms, and our
libraries, what feels right really *is* right.

I hope that these short poems will find short-term homes in the pockets of
many children and long-term homes in their memories. In or out of pockets,
the poems in this anthology reflect lives of contemporary children from
daybreak to bedtime, from schooltime to silly time. Kids will discover they
can swap poems with friends, perform them at assemblies, recite them for
grandparents, or give them away, again and again, without ever losing them.